The Fabian Society

The Fabian Society has played a central role for r
development of political ideas and public policy ....
the key challenges facing the UK and the rest of the industrialised world in a
changing society and global economy, the Society's programme aims to
explore the political ideas and the policy reforms which will define progressive
politics in the new century.

The Society is unique among think tanks in being a democratically-constituted
membership organisation. It is affiliated to the Labour Party but is editorially
and organisationally independent. Through its publications, seminars and
conferences, the Society provides an arena for open-minded public debate.

i

Fabian Society
11 Dartmouth Street
London SW1H 9BN
www.fabian-society.org.uk

 Fabian ideas
Series editor: Ellie Levenson

First published September 2002

ISBN 0 7163 0603 4
ISSN 1469 0136

British Library Cataloguing in Publication data.
A catalogue record for this book is available from the British Library.

Contents

Introduction   iv

1 | Beyond the 1945 settlement   1

2 | Learning from our history   7

3 | The case for collective provision   11

4 | Universal services, personalised provision   19

5 | The progressive prize   32

Introduction

I wanted to write this pamphlet to get across how important this political moment is for the left in Britain. Rarely in our history have we had such an opportunity to shape the political landscape and further our values. I am determined that we seize this opportunity.

The Labour Party is most successful when it has a reforming passion, unafraid to make the bold reforms necessary to meet new challenges. It is time to recognise that the 1945 settlement was a huge achievement but a product of that age and we today should not be its prisoners.

To deliver opportunity and security today, public services must be radically recast. Our challenge is to ensure that they are universal - an engine of equality; and personalised - responsive to the rising aspirations of the public. In short, universal services with personalised provision.

So this is a political pamphlet not a policy document. We are five years into our mission of public service reform. The foundations have been laid. As we step up the pace of reform it is right that we continue to state confidently the political case for change and the progressive prize if we achieve it.

Underlying it all is a single message: radical reform is the route to social justice. Only if we have the courage of our convictions and make the necessary changes will we be able to say that this Labour government lived up to the high ideals and practical achievements of the Government of 1945.

1| Beyond the 1945 settlement

I t is always harder to be critical about your own work than someone else's. So it is with the reform of our public services. Labour created the NHS, built the welfare state, and expanded educational opportunity to the many. These are our crown jewels and prize achievements, built by our political heroes and heroines; achievements shaped by our values but which required both vision and courage to see them through.

It's understandable, then, that to suggest that they are no longer always good enough and must be radically reformed can touch raw nerves. Yet we know in our hearts that if an ideal, no matter how worthy, fails to meet the challenge of the times it becomes a diminished ideal.

So let us start with a blunt truth. Our public services, despite the heroic efforts of dedicated public servants and some outstanding successes, are not all of the quality a nation like Britain needs.

There has been significant progress since 1997. Our primary schools are achieving the best ever results. Almost no infants are now in class sizes of over 30. There are 20,000 more teachers, 80,000 more school support staff and 39,000 more nurses. The number of heart operations each year has risen by a third since 1997. Fourteen new hospitals are open, 54 more are on the way -

the biggest hospital building programme in history. Overall crime is down 22 per cent since 1997 according to the comprehensive British Crime Survey.

There is much to be proud of. But we still have a long way to go before all our public services match the best international standards.

Too many criminals still go undetected and unpunished. While half of our 16-year olds achieve good qualifications, half do not - and tens of thousands of young people leave school each year with barely any qualifications at all. The NHS has recovered from the crisis of the early 1990s but maximum waiting times remain too long and standards of service too uneven. Our public transport system requires sustained investment and improvement.

We know this from our own experience, our constituents, from frontline staff, from policy experts, and from the statistics. And we also know the reason for these weaknesses is not just because public services have been starved of investment for decades, but also because they have not been reformed to deliver in a modern, consumer-focused fashion.

The aim of our reforms is to improve our public services, not to replace or dismantle them. We argue it must always be guided by our progressive values of opportunity, equality and responsibility, and by our enduring vision of economic and social progress. We want a Britain in which people can go as far as they have the talent to go, where prosperity and opportunity are widely shared. We favour true equality: equal worth and equal opportunity, not an equality of outcome focused on incomes alone. Strong, public services are fundamental to this vision of a fairer, more prosperous society.

To achieve our ambitions for our public services and the country, we must demonstrate the same courage and vision shown by Clement Attlee and Aneurin Bevan. Like them, we must challenge the status quo and refashion the public realm to meet the needs of our time. For now as then, universal public services are critical to combating poverty, and to promoting good health and education. But modern public services must also match modern expectations of quality and choice - not those of the 1940s.

No Labour supporter could be anything but proud of the first post-war Government's achievements. But it is time to acknowledge finally that the 1945 settlement was a product of its time and we must not be a prisoner of it. We must recognise that what was absolutely right for a time of real austerity no longer meets the needs and challenges in an age of growing prosperity and consumer demand.

Reform must, above all, help reconcile two impulses that pull individuals, society, and governments, in opposing directions. The first is individualism. A world in which there is more choice, more individualised services, more freedom to succeed - but which has bred greater insecurity if you are left to cope with these problems on your own or with inadequate skills and resources.

The other force is interdependence, a world moving closer together because of new technology and travel, a world where the problems of one part of the globe impact immediately on the other side. A world where we crave bonds of connection and the strengthening of solidarity in our society.

Modern public services - health, education, transport, law and order - need to reconcile this freedom of the individual to choose and the need for people to act together in solidarity.

The answer is to move beyond the 1945 settlement because the world has moved beyond the conditions of the immediate post-war era. The 1945 settlement was the social equivalent of mass production, when uniformity after decades of the 'welfare lottery' was an entirely worthy ambition. For good reasons, it was largely state-directed and managed, building a paternalistic relationship between state and individual, one of donor and recipient. Its aim was to provide a universal, largely basic and standardised service. Individual aspirations were often weak, and personal preferences were a low or non-existent priority. It was why there was some justification in the 'Whitehall knows best' attitude of the time.

This is no longer true, yet too often the old assumptions prevail. Today's population generally enjoy choice, quality, opportunity and autonomy on a scale never previously experienced. We should recognise and celebrate these new aspirations and expectations, much of it the consequence of the determination of Labour Governments to achieve a sustained increase in living standards for working people and their families.

Yet Labour understands that for all this progress, the need for active government and for strong public services remains today as crucial as ever. For we reject the Thatcherite claim that 'there is no such thing as society' with its policy response of cuts in funding leading to the run down of public services and the demoralisation of public servants.

We strongly believe that each of our public services is founded on the continuing need for collective provision. Crime and the fear of crime will only be tackled if we have a fully modernised police force and criminal justice system. There is no private market solution. Expanding educational opportunities, in a country still scarred by a lack of social mobility, requires collective provision if they are to benefit the many. So too with health care, when universal security and quality, in a time of rising drug bills, vastly improved medical technology and longer life expectancy, will never be achieved without collective provision. Not only are reformed public services essential to the vast majority of families in our country who could never afford to go private, they also advance social cohesion and are the means of addressing some of the most deep seated inequalities in Britain.

So we reject totally, as inefficient and unfair, a right wing philosophy of market choice for a few and 'sink services' for the many. But we also argue the case for moving beyond the outdated mass production approach that too often characterised public services after 1945.

We need to make our public services more responsive to local and individual needs. Customer satisfaction has to become a culture, a way of life, not an 'added extra'. That means national standards are necessary but not sufficient. Further devolution to the frontline, making services more responsive, is an essential next step.

The challenge is to invest in and improve our public services so they offer collective provision for all, tailored as far as possible to individual needs and preferences - universal services, personal provision. That means a Criminal Justice System rebalanced in favour of the victim. It means a National Health Service, but also a personal health service - not top down bureaucracy but locally responsive service. It means for schools , moving beyond the old, monolithic, 'one size fits all' system to a new specialist system with higher standards, better behaviour and more choice.

We should not be frightened of change or this challenge. On the left we believe in progress not the status quo. We have always been most successful when we have been most radical. We have faith, hope, and optimism about the future and a belief that political action can make life better for our fellow citizens. We believe that a reformed state can enhance individual opportunity and that 'private' is not always best. We have to prove that argument right and strengthen the consensus for it.

We have put the building blocks in place for a great progressive era in Britain: a new constitutional settlement, a stable and thriving economy in which people can plan ahead; more jobs, a minimum wage making work pay, more help for families and tax rises to pay for investment. But if we want to do more, to achieve a more equal society and more opportunity for those most in need, then we need to transform standards in our public services.

Now is the time to advance our vision. We have the potential to settle the political contours for generations to come; to establish a new consensus for our country that shifts the centre of gravity of British politics decisively in a progressive direction.

‟

2| Learning from our history

L abour is radical, not complacent, by instinct. Reforming, not conservative. We should learn from our history. When we are bold in pursuing reform, when we have a compelling vision and see it through, we are successful. When we simply defend the status quo, we fail and ultimately lose power.

Reform, change and progress are in our blood. In the early years of the Labour Party's history, our progressive mission demanded immediate action, right back to the first Labour Government's Wheatley Housing Act of 1924, to tackle the evils of homelessness and slum housing.

In the middle of the last century, Labour sought to combat the five giants of Want, Disease, Ignorance, Squalor and Idleness identified by Beveridge. The Attlee Government set in place a radically reformed framework of rights to employment, education, social insurance and healthcare. The 1945 settlement created a thirty-year consensus for the welfare state.

At the beginning of the 21st century we must continue to reform, so that our public services meet modern social needs and aspirations. Our goal, as always, is to empower the individual while ensuring fairness in access to public services. But how we do this changes from decade to decade and it is never easy.

The challenge of 1945 was to build a Britain of 'Fair Shares for

All' that would banish the poverty and unemployment of the inter-war years. The question people asked in 1945 was could life be different from the betrayal that so many soldiers and their families experienced after 1918? The Attlee Government faced economic difficulties more severe than any other. A currency crisis, industry destroyed by war, its export trade ruined. Britain was almost totally dependent on the United States for economic survival. Yet not once did that Government flinch from its progressive mission.

Successive Labour Chancellors in the 1940s, including Dalton, Cripps and Gaitskell, battled against formidable odds to find the resources to make social progress possible. Those resources were found. They fiercely rejected the old Treasury dogma that had done such damage to Britain's economy and society in the inter-war period and set out a plan for full employment and for a comprehensive health service and welfare state.

The Beveridge report was implemented. Pensions rose dramatically for widows and the elderly; family allowances were introduced for the first time. The 1945 Government brought in free secondary education opening up the possibility of university for more bright working-class pupils.

Each stage of reform was a battle. Nye Bevan took on not just the BMA in 1946-47, but also the Royal Colleges, local government and the British Medical Association to create the National Health Service in 1948. In the teeth of vociferous opposition he fought for Labour's ideals. The NHS was based on one solid founding principle: that health care should be given on the basis of a person's need not their wealth. Some objected to that principle then. Some would like us to abandon it today. Yet it was one of the greatest civilising acts of emancipation of the 20th century.

As Education Secretary, Tony Crosland sought to end the divisive 11-plus, and in the late 1960s Harold Wilson pursued the rapid expansion of higher education. In 1976 Jim Callaghan placed the issue of school standards firmly on the national agenda with his speech to Ruskin College, Oxford. These Labour leaders fought passionately for the right of every child to a decent education, rejecting the old Tory assumption that 'more always means worse' - that there is a small and fixed pool of talent in our country - which has long held Britain back and maintained class divisions.

Throughout its history our party has always struggled in the name of progress. Where we have been reformers, we have left great legacies. But where we have failed to reform despite the obvious case for it, we have paid a heavy price. Labour's failure in the 1960s and 1970s to reform the workings of industrial relations and the conduct of strikes aided the return of the Tories and their destructive policies. So too with Labour's failure in the 1970s to respond to the aspirations of many council tenants to own their own homes, which opened the way not just to 'right to buy' but to a wholesale Tory attack on local government and the provision of local services.

A genuine social partnership that accepts the need for change and reform is again essential for both Labour and the trade unions. The status quo is not sustainable without a step change in the quality and responsiveness of the public services.

Our task is to give modern expression to our values in a time of unprecedented aspirations, declining deference and increasing choice, of diverse needs and greater personal autonomy. We do so with Tony Crosland's concluding words to *The Future of Socialism* in mind: 'Socialist aspirations were first formulated over 100 years ago. Some remain urgently relevant...but of course new issues, not then foreseen, and increasingly important as the old evils are conquered, have arisen since; and they may be highly significant for welfare, freedom, and social justice'. That is the same reform imperative we confront today.

Other countries face the same challenges. Social democratic parties and governments across Europe have wrestled with the challenge of public service modernisation, and are progressing with bold policies to meet it. Sweden, Denmark and the Netherlands, for example, have promoted greater choice within the public health and education systems and are enforcing steadily higher national standards, including shorter maximum waiting times for hospital treatment and new rights for patients to access the private sector and go abroad where these times are not met.

An intense national debate on health and educational reform is taking place in Germany, amid concern about standards and efficiency, and all European countries are seeking to promote a wider diversity of pathways and institutions within their health and education systems. Reformist centre-left parties have nothing to fear from breaking down monolithic 'one size fits all' structures in the public services, when these are an obstacle to higher standards and aspirations. Like us, other reforming centre-left governments regard the restructuring of the public services, on the basis of principles similar to those we have set out, as vital to meeting traditional commitments to equality of opportunity and social justice in the modern world.

3| The case for collective provision

Britain's public services have suffered from long-term underinvestment. We have shown our commitment by substantial increases in investment including tax increases to fund a long-term strategy for renewing our public services. On the basis of economic strength and stability we are providing the resources needed to achieve high quality services for all. This investment is a source of bitter political controversy. But it is a battle of principle we must win.

Since 1945 public services have struggled against the financial instability of Britain's 'boom and bust' economy. They suffered neglect under the Tories in the 1950s. Not a single new hospital opened in Britain until the 1960s. In the 1960s and 1970s the numbers entering medicine and teaching oscillated as extra investment was committed and then cut back while economic conditions deteriorated. This led to severe staff shortages in schools and the NHS by the late 1970s.

These services then had to endure outright hostility from the Thatcher Governments of the 1980s. This meant lack of capital investment in public sector infrastructure; a consistently lower rate of earnings for professional public servants compared to the private sector and, by the late 1980s, real cuts across the public services. In the NHS spending continued to grow in real terms but at a lower rate than the 1960s and 1970s and in comparison to other industrial societies. The share of national income devoted to education fell significantly.

This steady squeeze on resources had a devastating impact on services. As the recent Wanless Report on the NHS revealed, over the last 20 years the number of nurses in the UK has increased by less than 20 per cent compared to a 65 per cent increase across the seven principal comparator countries. Britain has fewer doctors and nurses per head of population than these other countries as nurse and GP training places were cut back systematically under the Tories.

Against this background, growing disillusion and defensiveness among the millions of dedicated professionals who staff our public services were inevitable.

Much of the Tory dismantling was done under the guise of reform. One effect has been to make many in the public sector sceptical about change for fear that it will inflict further damage and undermine our public services even more. We acknowledge the need to explain change clearly to public service professionals, especially where it affects pay and employment conditions.

But under this Government reform is not a disguise for dismantling collective provision or declining employment standards but the route to higher standards. The commitment of public service staff is key to the delivery of high quality public services. We welcome developments in the NHS where the vast majority of staff who work for Public Finance Initiative (PFI) contractors in new hospitals will in future remain employed on NHS terms and conditions. Local government staff who transfer to private contractors through Best Value will have their terms and conditions fully protected under Transfer of Undertakings (Protection of Employment) Regulations (TUPE), including their pension rights, and new recruits will be employed on comparable terms and conditions of service. This Government will continue to safeguard employee interests through mandatory consultation and through dialogue with our colleagues in the public sector trade unions.

Public investment is now rising at unprecedented rates - 7.5 per cent a year real growth in health spending for the next five years, and 6 per cent real annual growth in education and social services spending for the next three years. This is only possible because of tough decisions taken in successive budgets. We are committed to significant ongoing increases in the rate of investment in our public services - faster than all other leading European countries in the case of health and education.

It has taken time to get to this position, but we need make no apologies. Since lasting improvement requires lasting investment it was essential to get the economy right first. We cannot make sustained investment in funding for schools, hospitals and rail without fiscal discipline. Cutting the national debt was a clear priority since servicing it cost us as much each year as the entire schools budget. Bank of England independence underpinned our commitment to stability avoiding a return to high interest rates and inflation. Lower unemployment meant higher tax receipts and reduced benefit costs.

Much of our first term strategy was hotly debated inside and beyond the party, including tough spending limits in our first two years in office, the windfall tax and the New Deal. But each of these policies was carefully designed to meet specific political and reform objectives, and the results speak for themselves.

I believe it will be the same in the second term. For example, we are committed to new methods for financing improvements to buildings and facilities in the public sector. A large proportion of Labour's investment in public services is direct public sector investment. Private sector investment through Public-Private Partnerships (PPP) is an addition to public sector investment rather than an alternative to it as it was under the Tories.

Each PPP is considered on its merits. There is no dogmatic attachment to private sector engagement for its own sake and there never will be. On this basis I believe the case for PPPs is now widely established and accepted on the progressive Left. There is nothing new in using the private sector to help modernise public sector infrastructure; every government has done so since 1945. In certain areas PPPs help increase investment tackling a massive backlog of neglect and desperately needed repairs. These PPP projects are also designed to transfer risk for construction delays and cost over-runs away from the taxpayer and towards private sector companies who have strong incentives as well as specialist skills to manage those risks. It is the private sector that is putting its capital at risk, and therefore the Government - more precisely taxpayers - do not have to bear all the risk in what are often highly complex infrastructure projects.

By instigating a competitive tendering process PPPs can also help to drive up cost efficiencies and encourage innovation in public service delivery. Public sector organisations are rightly encouraged to bid for management contracts, as they will with the new arrangements envisaged for failing schools and hospitals, but it is wrong to exclude the private sector if we are serious about innovation and service improvement.

Neither is a PPP a form of surrogate privatisation as our critics have alleged. With PPP most of the assets either remain or ultimately revert to the public sector: the Government is not 'selling off' hospitals or schools. The public sector continues to define the facilities it wants and to set and monitor service standards. It also retains the right to intervene if necessary to guarantee equity of access to services. But where a bid is of a higher quality and more cost effective we will use it. Ultimately the speedier delivery of service improvements that PPPs make possible, combined with examples of state of the art modernisation to our classrooms and operating theatres, strengthens public commitment to collective provision at a time of rising aspirations. We also have an obligation to provide the very best facilities for the staff in our public services.

PFI and PPP have been most controversial in the NHS, the London Underground and the Prison Service. Let me take them in turn: The biggest hospital building programme in the history of the NHS is under way. But with one third of NHS hospitals older than the NHS itself, conventional funding alone cannot deliver the investment that is needed. PFI has a central role to play in modernising the infrastructure of the NHS - but as an addition, not as an alternative to the substantial and increasing public sector capital programme. It is allowing more new NHS buildings to be built more quickly, providing high quality, patient-focused services out of modern, purpose designed buildings. PFI has delivered on time and within budget - something that public sector-led investment projects seldom managed to achieve. The National Audit Office has examined existing PFI schemes and found they will all deliver value for money - and this continues to improve. At the same time the public gains with a legal guarantee that each of these new hospitals must be maintained as never before throughout the lifetime of the PFI contract. In addition, we have ensured that at the end of the PFI contract, the NHS owns the hospital if that is in the best interests of the local health service.

Much controversy has surrounded the PPP for the London Underground. However, it is clear that we could not just carry on as before with an underfunded and deteriorating infrastructure under ever increasing pressure to meet growth in passenger travel in London. The PPP provides the best solution for London. The long term engineering contracts have secured an unprecedented commitment to fund the upgrades required - with a total expenditure of over £9 billion in the first 7 and a half years alone.

Strong incentives (and penalties) are in place to ensure that improvements are delivered on time and to budget. And independent evaluations have judged the contracts good value for money compared to the alternative of managing the work within the public sector, with all the risk of cost overruns that have dogged previous major projects.

The experience of the Prison Service, where PFI has been in use for more than a decade, bears out many of these points. Over the last seven years, seven new prisons have been constructed and operated by the private sector. This is a small proportion of the total. But the record of private sector engagement has been beneficial not only in the value for money of individual projects, but also in precipitating major improvements in the way that public prisons are operated with considerable efficiency gains. As a result the public sector has raised its game significantly, to the point where the Prison Service has been able to win back business from the private sector. The Director-General of the Prison Service has argued strongly that the impact of engagement with the private sector has led to improved standards and efficiency in the public sector.

As a result of our investment programme, Britain is the only European country where public spending as a proportion of national income in education and health will rise this year and next, taking Britain to 5.6 per cent in education and 8.7 per cent in health by 2006 and closing the gap with average European levels of funding. In the recent Comprehensive Spending Review we set out our bold spending plans for public services with schools and hospitals first. Together with the boldest programme of reform for fifty years, our aim is to achieve significant improvements in public service performance with rising consumer satisfaction.

This is a far cry from 1979 when the Thatcher Government declared in line one of their first public spending White Paper that: 'Public expenditure is at the heart of Britain's present economic difficulties'. The legacy of the Tory years is chronic under-capacity. There are too few trained teachers and doctors, pay in the public sector still lags significantly behind other private sector professions, and the infrastructure and facilities are often out of date let alone state of the art.

The investment we are putting in is a basic precondition for achieving a world-class NHS and education system and a truly effective Criminal Justice system. But we have to be realistic.

We are going to make significant improvements in the health service; but we are not going to complete its renewal within the term of this Parliament. It takes three years to train a nurse, around seven years to train a doctor and yet longer for a combination of training and experience to produce a competent consultant. Neither is it possible to upgrade the rail system quickly as massive infrastructure projects take years to complete, or to transform performance in our schools overnight. These all require investment and reform, feeding through to progressively higher standards. Above all, we have to be honest in accepting that increased investment alone will not solve the problems we face. The challenge for us is to combine investment and reform in an indissoluble union, public service by public service.

PPPs, as outlined above, are only one aspect of our reform strategy, and in most areas by no means the most significant. More important is improving, and in many areas transforming the public sector iself. Our strategy to achieve this is set out in the next chapter - based on the four principles of public service reform I set out after the last election: national standards, devolution of power to the front-line, a new deal for public service staff, and greater choice. These principles are increasingly well understood by the innovators within public services. It is now vital that across the Labour movement we expound this strategy with clarity and conviction.

But it is equally essential that the four principles, and the programmes flowing from them, be seen for what they are: a means to an end, not the end in itself. Policies to promote leadership and public-private partnership, tackle service failure, modernise working practices and promote accountability are not the raison d'etre of this Labour Government. They are simply some among many ways in which we will achieve our mission to create world class public services meeting the needs of the individual citizen within a strong, cohesive society.

4| Universal services, personalised provision

Our goal is public services offering the choice and quality demanded by the modern citizen, and doing so universally, not simply for a minority as in the past. It means quality services with no-one left behind. Services that are characterised by the flexibility, choice and responsiveness that people have grown accustomed to in other parts of their lives, but not at the expense of what makes public services special: that they are available to all on the basis of citizenship and need, not the ability to pay. Modern public services need to affirm our status as citizens, while meeting our demands as consumers.

This will only be achieved by transforming the Attlee settlement. This is partly a matter of social change: Attlee governed in the shadow of a devastating war when expectations were a world apart from today. But it also involves a change in political outlook. In the 1940s expectations of the state as the universal provider of efficient public services were high but largely untried by experience. The liberal socialist tradition, stretching back to Robert Owen and TH Green, emphasising localism, devolution and mutualism, was downplayed in the quest for rapid national consolidation in a post-war period when the voluntary and private sectors were weak, unable to rise to the challenge.

The courage of our convictions

Our task today is to use the additional investment made available by successful economic management to shape public services that meet modern consumer expectations. Even in the worst crises of Tory under-investment and neglect, the best public services were outstanding. Our best state schools, universities and hospitals have always achieved as well or better than those in the private sector and their international counterparts, despite less funding. Dedicated public service staff, triumphing over poor conditions and intense pressure, built beacons of excellence in every sector.

Labour's task in government is to spread this excellence universally, extending quality and choice rapidly as investment and capacity increase, strengthening opportunity and security for all our people.

Our four principles of public service reform are the means to succeed. They are simply stated:

- Guaranteed national standards of service
- Devolution of power and innovation to the front line
- A new deal for public service staff, combining better rewards for increased professionalism.
- Greater choice for the consumer

No one of these four principles is sufficient alone. Each is vital. High standards will become universal only if each local manager - each headteacher, each hospital chief executive, and each police superintendant - takes real responsibility for the quality and character of their service. Equally, high national standards and greater choice are not possible without better trained and rewarded professional staff, and more flexible staff working practices. Choice is crucial both to individual empowerment and - by enabling the consumer to move to an alternative provider where dissatisfied - to quality of service. Yet more choice without high national standards will result, inevitably, in choice only for a minority, as under the Tories. Furthermore, in some areas choice is necessarily limited or non-existent, so quality cannot always be driven by the option to change supplier, however effective elsewhere. Success therefore requires reform across a broad front, with no pretence that there is a single prescription or policy to cure each problem.

Let me say more about the four principles and what they mean in terms of sustaining change and improvement across our public services.

National standards driving equality

For the first time in history, we have established a national framework of standards and accountability with floor targets beneath which no public service should fall. Accountable public bodies must uphold these standards, with effective intervention powers in cases of failure. These national standards are essential to break down regional and local disparities in access to provision and to ensure poor quality provision is tackled. Some people argue that national standards are unnecessary. But I say that without them we sacrifice equality and fail to guarantee quality. Decades of experience bear this out.

It is right and necessary that variations in public service standards should be exposed to consumers. We know it is often the case that poorer people suffer the poorest service standards. That is no longer acceptable. Few now question the value of regular independent inspection of standards in schools and the publication of test and exam results. We have extended the publication of results school by school, improving accountability to parents and local communities. For hospitals, we have created an independent standards inspectorate from scratch, and have also strengthened the accountability regime for the railways and the standards regime for the police.

Government's job is to define basic acceptable standards, ensuring they are met and properly resourced. In education, for example, literacy and numeracy are the indispensable foundations of success at school. When we came to power in 1997, nearly half of primary school leavers were behind the standard expected of their age - a terrible indictment of the education system. Investment and support - including the national literacy and numeracy strategies, and funding to reduce infant class sizes to 30 or less - have helped teachers transform standards. Primary school results are now the best ever. A rigorous approach is now being taken to the critical challenge of ensuring high basic standards in secondary schools, not only in the teaching of English and maths but also in securing basic good conduct and behaviour, including a sustained assault on truancy. The national service frameworks are fulfilling a similar role in the NHS, tackling the 'postcode lottery'. These are now in place for heart and cancer treatment, mental health and services for older people; they will soon be extended to diabetes and children's services.

As we invest, standards must rise and the definition of minimum acceptable standards needs to rise sharply. In health we are setting steadily more demanding targets for reducing maximum waiting times for hospital treatment - reducing the maximum year by year from 18 months last year to six months by 2005 for in-patients. Waiting is the curse of the NHS. It is essential that short maximum waiting times - shorter even than six months beyond 2005 - are achieved and enforced nationally, with whatever redress is necessary for those not treated in time by their local NHS suppliers. A similar approach to basic national standards is being taken in the public transport and criminal justice sectors.

Letting go - devolution to the front line

National standards are necessary but not remotely sufficient to provide good quality services. They are a way of ensuring minimum thresholds of provision but not enough to achieve universal excellence and consumer responsiveness. For that to happen power must be devolved with incentives and consumer pressure brought to bear at local level.

So within a framework of national standards and accountability, there must be far more devolution of power and responsibility to the front line. Those in charge of local service provision - headteachers, GPs, nurses, police superintendants, hospital chief executives - freed from red tape and empowered to innovate to meet local demands. We recognise and understand the need to let go and release the energy and commitment that pervade so many public service organisations.

The evidence is overwhelming that front-line leadership makes a critical difference to the quality of public services. Without a good headteacher, a school will drift or fail. Good headteachers and management teams lead outstandingly successful schools in even the toughest areas. Our reforms are geared to strengthening local leadership - to give effective headteachers and their governors, and successful hospital managers and their trusts, real control over their institutions and a mission to innovate boldly, subject to proper accountability. Local leadership is equally important in health, policing and local authority provided services such as housing, where effective estate-level management is essential to meet tenant demands.

We are pushing through radical changes to achieve this. Nearly 90 per cent of school funding now goes straight into school budgets, and we are increasing direct funding further still. Within the NHS, 75 per cent of funding will from 2004 go directly to the new local Primary Care Trusts so they can provide and fund the services needed for their locality. The number of health authorities is being reduced sharply, and their powers reduced. We are also keen to see devolution of police funding to local 'basic command units' where this makes operational sense.

But we need to go further still. New powers to encourage school expansion, takeover and federations will further empower successful school leaders. A new category of City Academies is being established - fully independent schools run by their sponsors and governing bodies, subject to agreeing key service standards with the government. Top performing hospitals are asking for greater autonomy so that they can operate as not-for-profit trusts able to develop their services free from central direction. At the other end of the spectrum, poor hospitals will not be left to sink or swim as in the old internal market. The National Institute for Clinical Excellence (NICE), with support from the Modernisation Agency and inspection by the new Commission for Healthcare Audit and Inspection (CHAI) work to ensure that all hospitals provide decent standards of care.

I readily accept that there may be tension between guaranteed national standards, the machinery to underpin and enforce them, and the freedom necessary for local autonomy and diversity to flourish. In many areas this tension is marginal or non-existent, because guaranteed national standards are achieved and taken for granted. No successful teacher or GP or hospital manager is clamouring for the freedom to fail their pupils or patients and all have considerable flexibility to develop their services within the national framework of basic standards and accountability.

However, I recognise that the red tape surrounding accountability regimes can be unnecessarily burdensome and restrictive. Hence our intention to extend 'earned autonomy'; a right for the successful who are achieving good standards to manage their affairs and innovate with greater freedom from central oversight and red tape. Foundation hospitals, and the reduced Ofsted obligations on highly rated schools, are examples of this. We intend to take 'earned autonomy' further in the next phase of reform.

The related issue of local control and accountability is also important. It is wrong to suggest a necessary conflict between national and local oversight. Local authorities and local electors have no more interest than good headteachers and hospital managers in sustaining failing services. In areas where they are themselves responsible for service provision, local authorities recognise the importance of national standards alongside local autonomy as a spur enabling them to procure improvements at service level. Nonetheless, the balance between national and local government is a legitimate issue of debate. The Local Government White Paper has proposed new freedoms and flexibilities for local authorities, and we are open to proposals to further local authority innovation to improve local services and accountability.

Our commitment to earned autonomy contrasts sharply with the Tory vision of a 'new localism'. Their rhetoric may have changed to a more localist and compassionate tone. But the reality has not changed. Their 'localist' vision goes hand-in-hand with a determination to cut funding. It is not intended to empower localities, but to escape from national obligations to provide adequate investment and guaranteed standards.

Reform of the professions: the route to a renewed public service ethos

A new professionalism is a crucial aspect of our reform agenda. How do we encourage professionals to be consumer focused, responding to the personalised and often strong wishes of vociferous customers, and yet at the same time retain the very ethos that makes our public services so special?

At its best the notion of public service embodies vital qualities - loyalty, altruism, dedication, long term relationships with users, a sense of pride. It is an ethos that is the motivating force

25

to make a nurse stay late with a patient in distress. It is the same ethos that makes a teacher strive over many years to improve the chances of a child who finds learning difficult. And the public know too that they are more than consumers of public servants, but citizens too. A patient in A&E demanding his hand is stitched up acts as a consumer fuming at the delay. But when he sees a car crash victim rush past him on a trolley he acts as a citizen, understanding that a more urgent case comes first.

So public services will never be just another customer service. Yet too often public sector employers and the government have taken the dedication of public servants for granted. In the 1960s and 1970s the rapid rate of expansion of public services made it difficult for that ethos to be applied to each individual user. As a result public service to many became a less appealing vocation.

So the public service ethos came under pressure. It no longer seemed such a great calling. The pressures too great, the rewards too little. People have different expectations of our public servants. Government rightly pushes for higher standards, the public rightly push for faster, more responsive services.

I realise the huge task we have to renew the spirit within our public services - and I believe the way to achieve it is by reforming the professions so that people feel more fulfilled, more able to cope with the growing demands placed upon them. Once again radical reform, I believe, is the solution and not the problem.

I believe that only if we give our public servants the tools to respond to these new demands will we be able to bolster the ethos we all believe in. So a modernised workforce is essential to providing modern public services. Employees in the public sector must be allowed to break away from out-dated systems.

It means better pay and conditions. This year and last, public sector salaries were growing at a faster rate than private sector salaries for the first time in twenty years. We are introducing a range of bursaries, grants and raising starting pay for teachers, doctors and nurses.

From April 2001 the Government introduced its Starter Homes Initiative with funding of £250 million over the period 2001-2004 to assist public sector workers in buying homes. The numbers of people employed in public services has increased by around 200,000 since 1997. There are now more teachers in maintained schools than at any time in the last twenty years, and we have funded repairs to 17,000 schools. There are 39,000 more nurses and midwives and 10,000 more doctors. The NHS plan provides for 7,000 extra beds by 2004.

We offer a new partnership to frontline staff that could herald a renaissance in the esteem and effectiveness of public service - a new public service ethos. For our part we offer more investment, more recruitment, better pay and conditions, and new career opportunities. In return we expect high standards of professional engagement, and we seek a new flexibility in the professions that break down old working practices, old demarcations.

This means tackling the outdated systems and practices that demoralise staff, prevent them using their skills to the full and which undermine their efforts to improve services.

So we must use the investment provided to help them work more effectively. We need reforms to prevent consultants having to waste time because of the way their clinics are run, and doctors and teachers having to complete most paperwork by hand. The introduction of classroom assistants and bursars into schools will free teachers and heads to focus on their primary responsibilities. The greater use of use of computers and support staff, already being piloted in 30 schools, will cut preparation and marking time, as will the provision of extra training and profes-sional development opportunities. We want to use clerical staff in police stations to take on the form filling which soaks up on average eight hours a week of police officers' time.

All this shows our commitment to improving our public services and in investing in our public servants. It is understandable that, after many years in which the Conservatives' talk of reform masked a programme of cuts and worsening job conditions, public service employees are sometimes suspicious of reform now. But I hope we can convince them that the reform programme we are embarked upon, with its increased resources, represents an opportunity, not a threat. We know that the morale of staff is a critical factor in the quality of public services; we are determined to uphold and improve it.

Choice

Choice is an important principle for our reform programme. We need far more choice - not only *between* public service suppliers but also *within* each public service. Where appropriate, choice enhances quality of provision for the poorest, helping to tackle inequalities, while it also strengthens the middle-class commitment to collective provision.

In education, greater choice means choice *between* schools, so that more parents can choose a school that fully meets their child's needs. Often this will be the nearest school; but sometimes it will be a school further afield, for its higher standards or for some special aspect of its ethos or provision.

We therefore need far more schools which parents want to choose. Hence our desire to see successful schools expand and take over weak or failing schools. New legislation to encourage successful schools to expand, and to facilitate school takeovers and new federations, will allow steadily more parents to secure their school of choice. So too will the establishment of entirely new City Academies in areas of poor achievement. Hence also our policy for every secondary school - not a minority as in the past - to develop a distinctive character and real centre of specialist excellence, in addition to its teaching of the full national curriculum. These 'specialist schools' - with specialisms in areas including enterprise, modern languages, sport, technology and the arts - will account for more than half of all secondary schools by 2005, generating more good secondary schools and a greater capacity to choose between schools. We want every secondary school on a clear ladder of improvement, becoming specialist not merely in a technical sense but with a character and an ethos that is distinctive to each school and that focuses on the talent and potential of each child.

But we also need more choice *within schools*, particularly in the later secondary years as the talents and aspirations of pupils diverge. This requires a modernised curriculum with much better pathways for vocational and work-related studies. It also requires a broader range of provision, with every school offering serious sporting and cultural opportunities to their pupils. Better post-16 provision, with greater choice of courses within 6th forms and between school 6th forms and colleges, is also vital. Every secondary school needs to change to meet these requirements, offering more and better choices to their pupils, tailored to their individual talents.

In health, there is a similar imperative to increase choice within and between services. People living increasingly busy lives want far greater choice of access to the NHS - evening and weekend surgeries, NHS Direct, walk-in centres, and greatly improved A&E departments able to cope with more routine incidents quickly. Greater choice between NHS-funded suppliers is also needed, to satisfy individual requirements and to meet guaranteed waiting times for operations where local suppliers are unable to do so. Heart surgery patients now have a wider choice of treatment - in hospitals nationwide, in the private sector, and even abroad - if they have been waiting more than six months, and we intend to spread this policy across the NHS. New freestanding diagnostic and treatment centres, specialising in particular conditions such as cataracts, will enhance choice. By 2005 all patients will be able to book a convenient time and place for their treatment at the point they are referred to hospital by a GP.

All these policies expand choice for the many, not just the minority who are able to exercise choice by opting-out and paying for their school or operation or utilising private insurance.

Extending choice in these ways involves new forms of engagement with the voluntary and private sectors. We will intensify this process as required to expand choice for the many. We are keen, for example, to engage more private hospitals and overseas suppliers, and more voluntary or private sector managers of schools, to provide state-funded services as long as this remains within a national framework guaranteeing access to all on the basis of need and the capacity to benefit, not the ability to pay.

The political stakes in this reform programme could not be higher. No-one expects overnight transformation. But the electorate must see reform and improvement advancing resolutely, meeting new consumer demands, and generating steadily more services of choice and greater public confidence that acceptable standards will be met nationwide. Only on this basis will we carry the support necessary to increase investment - or indeed to remain in power at all. If we fail, the alternative neo-liberal agenda of privatisation and opting out of public services will assert itself.

Already, in some parts of the country up to a fifth of all routine surgery is carried out privately. In London, 17 per cent of parents use independent schools; and half of all A-levels are taken outside the maintained sector. The basis for a substantial further advance in privatised provision is there if public services do not match rising expectations.

In health and schooling, collective funding through taxation is the fairest and most efficient way of providing a universal service. But that does not mean that all healthcare provision and schools have to be owned and controlled directly by the state. In Germany around 40 per cent, Belgium around 60 per cent and in the Netherlands over 80 per cent of hospitals providing public healthcare are independent not-for-profits, similar to the foundation hospitals we are now proposing here. We propose to take forward this concept as set out in our post-budget health reform plan. Foundation hospitals will be independent, not-for-profit institutions, broadly similar to hospitals in many other parts of Europe, with operational freedom combined with much stronger representation of the community interest. They will enable communities to reclaim a stake in their local hospitals as they will be directly accountable to a 'stakeholder board' rather than to Whitehall officials. Similarly, a wide diversity of excellent schools, with real autonomy, can make an important contribution to higher standards and wider opportunities for the many.

Britain is in the mainstream of modern social democratic thinking in promoting public service reform to secure higher standards, diversity and choice.

5| The progressive prize

New Labour's purpose is not simply to amend a few policies or to manage the country more efficiently. It is to set a new course for Britain in the 21st century. Central to this goal is the transformation of our public services.

We reject the pessimists and the Tories who believe our public services cannot be improved and increasing investment would only be pouring more money into a bottomless pit. Their option is privatised services for the better off and cheap 'safety net' public services for the poor with dismantled protection for those who work in them. It is a future of extremes in which the divide between rich and poor grows as the middle-class opts out systematically from public provision. The goal is a smaller state with an ever-decreasing share of national income invested in public services.

It is why they spend so much time denigrating our public services, refusing to acknowledge progress, desperate to demoralise those who work in them and those who use them. What they want to do is to undermine the notion of universal public service, paid for through taxes and based on need not ability to pay.

We reject also the view, held by some on the Left, that a Labour Government's role is simply to defend existing services, not to extend choice or accountability but simply pour in more money.

They share - although they would never admit it - the Right's pessimistic view that our public services cannot fully meet people's needs and aspirations. They believe - wrongly in my view - that the best way to defend those working in the public service and to secure their futures is to defend the status quo and veto reform. This approach urges higher public spending to address the worst shortcomings of current provision, but would leave arcane structures in the public sector largely unchanged.

Radical Investment and Reform

New Labour, in contrast, is confident in our public services and public servants. Our vision is rooted in strong public services that extend social justice in a dynamic market economy through investment in the talents of every individual, not just an elite.

We believe public services are both a ladder of opportunity and a source of security in a global economy, helping our citizens to negotiate unpredictable change. So we are prepared not only to inject greater investment into public services, but to ensure they can play their full part in building a fairer society, to reform the systems and structures of those services for the modern era.

The opportunity for the centre-left in British politics to shape the destiny of the country has never been greater. But if the Right is able to claim through our inability to reform these institutions or promote choice for the individual citizen that public services are inherently flawed, we will see support for them wither and the clamour for private provision increase. It will mean a further assault on the public realm and a devastating attack on our most cherished ideals.

By contrast, if we are bold enough in our mission to reform we will rehabilitate public services after two decades of neglect, and mark not merely a new advance for progressive politics, but the extension of opportunity and social justice in our society. This represents a great and precious moment for Britain.

We recognise we cannot achieve this alone. To be strong incumbents supporting the public sector while also acting as agents of change, is an inherently difficult task. It requires a government able to learn and renew as it governs. We must improve the partnership with the people who work in our public services and those who use them. The political and intellectual resources to sustain a progressive government extend well beyond our own party confines, and we need to exploit those resources more effectively.

On 4 June 1944, two days before the D-Day landings, Churchill invited Ernie Bevin to accompany him to Portsmouth to say farewell to some of the troops. 'They were going off to face this terrific battle', Bevin recounted, 'with great hearts and great courage. The one question they put to me as I went through their ranks was: 'Ernie, when we have done this job for you are we going back on the dole? Both the Prime Minister and I answered 'No, you are not'.

The people in 1945 wanted a government that could fulfil their hopes of work and dignity in old age, of decent life-chances for their children. Half a century later in a time of peace and prosperity we again have the chance to advance decisively the interests of working people and their families in Britain.

Only by meeting this urgent challenge of revitalising our public services can we realise Labour's historic values. Strong public services have always defined New Labour's purpose, infused our ambition, and fuelled our optimism about what we can achieve for Britain in the 21st century. It would be a betrayal of our Party's past achievements and values if we were to falter in the task of reform. For reform is the surest route to social justice.